WRITTEN & ILLUSTRATED
BY CHARLIE O'SHIELDS

doodlewash BOOKS

doodlewash.com

Copyright © 2022 Charlie O'Shields

All rights reserved. No part of this book may be reproduced in any form or by any electronic or mechanical means, including information storage and retrieval systems, without written permission from the author, except for the use of brief quotations in a book review. For more information, address: letspaint@doodlewash.com.

DOODLEWASH is a registered trademark of Storywize, LLC.
All Rights Reserved.

ISBN 978-1-7371806-0-9 (Hardcover)
ISBN 978-1-7371806-1-6 (Paperback)

Everyone Can Draw!

We were all born with the ability to make art from the moment we could first hold a crayon. We instinctively knew how to draw and color. This natural instinct to see and recreate the world around us is a rather magical thing indeed! Sort of like something you might only expect from a wizard or a magician. Well, that's exactly what YOU become whenever you doodle, sketch or draw! So, let's make some magic together!

Charlie O

Let's Begin!

Why hello there my friend! I'm so thrilled you're here!
You have magical powers that will soon become clear.
There's a mystery to solve, and some things are in doubt,
so I'll need your great talents to figure it all out.

You'll just need a wand, at the ready and extended.
A pencil, pen, or crayon, will all be quite splendid!
Are you ready? Oh good! There's a box just below.
Make some scribbles with your wand! Just give it a go!

PSSSST HINT: Choose something to draw with that doesn't bleed through to the other side of the paper!

Wasn't that fun?
Yes, it's quite easy to DO!
All the skills that you need,
are right there inside you!
You see, a scribble is always
a wonderful start!
As the best magic comes
from inside your heart.

Are you pleased with the wand
that you've chosen my friend?
If you're not, try another,
and then we'll begin.

Wand At The Ready?

Oh that's great! How sublime!
Now, let's start our story
as we draw upon a time!

One Little Ghost

Once upon a time,
I was floating all alone.
I truly wasn't certain
as to just which way I'd blown.

There were some scary creatures
I saw moving down the street.
I'm just one little ghost, you see,
who happens to be sweet.

I hear you have magical powers.
See things others can't!
And only you can see me now,
so my options are quite scant.

There's something spooky out there
and it's giving me a fright!
I hope that you will help to keep me safe
throughout the night.

You have a look upon your face
like you've just seen a ghost!
But if you get to know me,
I'll be the ghost you like the most!

I'm not one to shriek or scream
whenever folks come near.
I know if we spend time together,
that will be quite clear.

But, I'm also a wee bit shy,
and we've not met like we should.
Meeting a brand new friend is
always wonderful and good!

So, perhaps we should begin
by playing a little game.
Let's test that magic wand
and see if you can **GUESS MY NAME!**

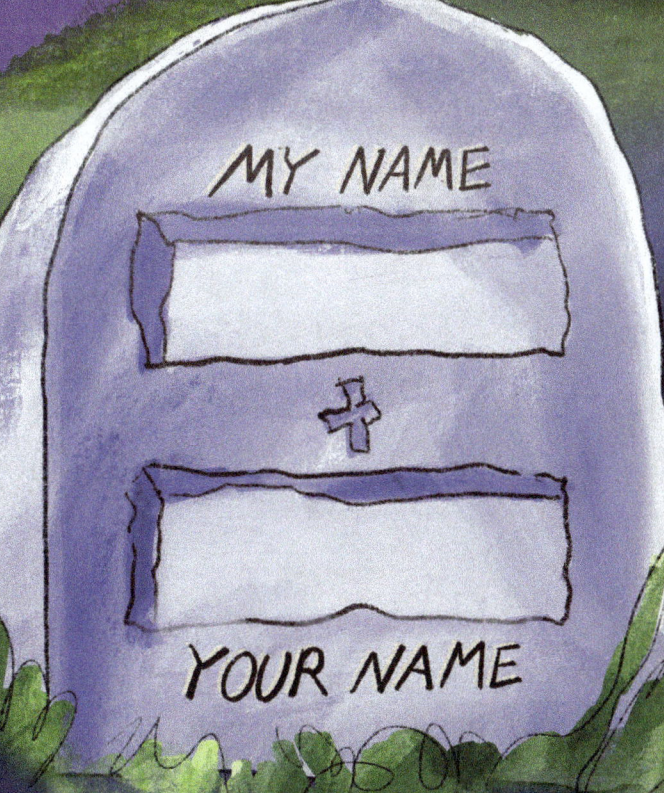

Wow! That's exactly right!
I'm not sure how you knew.
That's quite a clever trick!
What a treat to be with you!

I've always been a bit frightened
doing things I haven't tried.
When I'm faced with something new,
I sort of want to hide.

Sometimes I think I'm not
that good at anything I do.
I worry I might mess things up
and never make it through.

Though, I guess that being perfect
would make life such a bore.
If I had all I ever wanted,
I might not wish for more.

But the path is very dark,
and those creatures are still there!
I think that if you joined me,
we would make a perfect pair.

I've been floating all alone, you see,
so I'm super glad you're here.
You make me feel so safe
as though there's nothing left to fear.

DRAW WHAT THE GHOST SAW!

Let's move on and see
what we can find along the way.
I know that you've just met me,
but I really hope you'll stay.

Look!
There's something on the ground
that always comes in handy
I really can't believe my luck!
It's my **FAVORITE CANDY!**

Yes indeed! That's it!
Candy is such a wonderful treat!
I never have it often,
which is why it's just so neat!

I think about that sometimes
as I'm floating through the air.
The things in life that matter most
are often the most rare.

In truth, I've never seen
another ghost before, you see.
I'm sure there must be others,
but for now, it's only me.

Maybe one day when I'm older,
that ghost and I will meet.
They will know I'm so much more
than something floating in a sheet.

DRAW WHAT THE GHOST SAW!

Wait! Did you hear that sound?
It came from over there!
I know you're likely thinking
I'm the easy one to scare.

That's true, of course, but I try each day
to be a bit more brave.
I think I have all I'd ever want,
but it's courage I still crave.

Yet there it is again!
What on earth has caused that sound?
Oh yikes! There's something crawling
over there upon the ground!

Oh dear! I can do this!
I just have to open
my eyes a bit wider.
Why, it's not a monster after all,
it's only a **LITTLE SPIDER!**

I've often heard that spiders
tend to cause a bit of fright.
But, when they're left alone,
they rarely ever bite.

I guess it's true for many creatures,
at least those that I've seen.
Most are perfectly nice and lovely,
and there's no reason to be mean.

But those creatures that I saw before
were of a different kind.
They were more like monsters,
which is why they're on my mind.

I'm determined to find out for sure,
though, now that I have you!
You have that magic wand,
and I can make an alarming **"BOO!"**

Oh no! I think I made you jump!
That was really not my aim.
I just wanted you to know
that I'm so happy that you came!

Eek! Look over there!
Going that way won't be wise.
I think we're being watched
by all those super SPOOKY EYES!

DRAW WHAT THE GHOST SAW!

Let's hurry on! If those eyes have bodies,
I really don't want to see!
It seems that so many creatures I find,
are often larger than me.

I've always wished I could be bigger,
but being small is fine.
It's just the way I'm meant to be...
Oh look! I see a sign!

It says "This Way to Monster Manor."
Well, that doesn't sound so scary.
Yes, of course, I'm only kidding!
We should really be more wary!

Maybe we should turn around
and head in the other direction.
I'm not quite sure that even a wand
could offer the right protection.

Oh no! But then there are those
spooky eyes we left back there.
Sometimes decisions can be tough.
This doesn't feel quite fair.

You have that look upon your face
like you're curious and want to see.
Yet my sheet is really shaking
and I think that we should flee!

I can't seem to convince you that
we really should head back?
Well, I don't believe you'd ever
lead me down a harmful track.

Okay, but before we go and put
your wild plan in motion,
I think that first, we should
examine this bottle of MAGIC POTION!

DRAW WHAT THE GHOST SAW!

That's amazing! And perhaps
this potion will help us too!
If nothing else, it's certainly
a rather thrilling clue.

I wonder who left this here?
I hope that we're not hexed!
I guess we'll have to venture on
to find what happens next.

I've never been good with magic.
You seem to know much more.
And the way you wield that wand,
you always know just what's in store.

I was told something about that once,
which I thought was rather smart.
That real magic is just a hopeful glow
you carry inside your heart.

Though in this creepy forest,
I'm not sure just what is true.
Nothing is as it seems here.
I'm not certain of what to do.

Let's move on and see if we can
sort out what's this or that.
Like that object lying there!
Oh my, it's a **POINTY HAT!**

Draw what the ghost saw!

I think I've seen a hat like that,
but I'm not completely sure.
Perhaps it's all just a clever trap!
Something meant to lure!

I really hope we don't find any
more of those spooky goods.
We shouldn't have come this far
into these creepy woods!

DRAW WHAT THE GHOST SAW!

And yet I spy something else,
over there upon the ground.
I think we should move quietly
and try not to make a sound.

Wait, I thought it was a face at first,
but now I have to ask,
Is it something else?
Why yes! It's a rather SPOOKY MASK!

Whoa! I wonder who would wear
such a thing upon their face?
I guess there are many mysteries
that we'll find inside this place.

I've almost forgotten about
those scary creatures that I met.
It seems there could be other things
that just might be a threat!

I think we should take a moment
to rethink just where we're going.
Do you really want to see monsters?
It's true. My fear is showing.

But, maybe instead we could take
a little break over by that light.
Yikes! It's a JACK-O-LANTERN!
It gave me such a fright!

DRAW WHAT THE GHOST SAW!

Well, that pumpkin is really fun
and not super scary at all!
I shouldn't be so quick to fear,
even though I'm small.

While it's good to have some caution
if things are not quite clear,
when you take the time to learn a bit,
there's often less to fear.

Oh no! We've reached the house!
There are surely monsters there!
I don't think it's wise to enter!
We really shouldn't dare!

I know I seem to keep expecting
only gloom and doom.
But look there on the ground!
I think it's **A MAGIC BROOM!**

DRAW WHAT THE GHOST SAW!

I see you're quite the curious type
and want to go inside.
Are you sure you wouldn't rather
find a lovely place to hide?

No, you say? You really want to
see what's behind that door?
Oh my! I guess we've come this far,
so we might as well explore.

I'll just cover up my eyes and
you can tell me what you see.
I know it might seem silly, but then
I won't be so quick to flee.

It smells really musty here!
This place must be super old.
And there seems to be a draft!
It really is quite cold!

I think that we should leave now
before those monsters come.
I don't think we'd be welcome.
I'm not meaning to be glum.

I'm sure they must be the creatures
I saw roaming down the street.
And, I don't think that they're
the kind that I would like to meet.

So, this was fun, but let's get out of here
as quickly as we can.
I wanted to solve this mystery,
but realize now I had no plan.

You seem disappointed
as if you want to see some more.
You probably want to know
what's lurking behind that door.

Well, since you have your wand,
I guess we should be fine.
I feel you know just what to do,
were we to cross that line.

But it really is quite dark in here
so before you turn that handle,
I think we should prepare a bit.
We definitely need this **CANDLE!**

DRAW WHAT THE GHOST SAW!

Wow!
There's a table filled with treats.
That's quite a monster feast.
Perhaps it's meant to trick us!
We'll be captured by some beast!

Though it does seem more like
there's a party happening here.
Yet just where all the guests
have gone is not completely clear.

They haven't touched their cookies
or their strangely purple pie!
And the only thing we've seen so far
is a cat who likes to spy.

I think that I should understand,
but don't quite feel I'm able.
Why on earth are there **BALLOONS**
floating by the table?

DRAW WHAT THE GHOST SAW!

This night is getting stranger and
the clues don't make much sense.
I feel this place is not as it seems
and it's making me so tense.

I thought I could be braver,
but now, don't even want to look.
Perhaps I'll just distract myself
by reading this strange book.

WOAH!
That book must have been magic
and now I'm somewhere new.
I'm not sure what this place is,
and I've lost sight of you!

Oh dear! I guess it's true then.
I just can't do anything right.
I've made a mess of everything,
and now my friend is out of sight.

It's been so many years now
that I've been floating on my own.
I guess this is really nothing new.
It's truly all I've known.

But in my soul, I've always thought
that there was something more.
Perhaps I'd find some other ghosts,
and together we would soar!

Wait! That book is still over there!
I wonder what it's for?
And though I'm not entirely sure,
I feel like I've seen it before.

And next to it, I see a wand.
Maybe I'll make some magic too!
But, I'm not like my friend.
I never know just what to do!

There are words written on the page,
but nothing in the middle.
Indeed, I think I get it now!
It must be some kind of riddle!

"A symbol most powerful,
where all real magic finds its start"
Yes! I think I know the answer now!
It's most definitely a heart!

I'm back! And there you are my friend!
I found a wand and was able to draw!
And, I see you've found something, too.
Those are the monsters that I saw!

Oh no! They're going to eat us now!
Ugh! I think I'm going to be sick.
We've got to get ourselves out of here!
Make our exit and be quick!

What's that look upon your face?
Why aren't you starting to run?
Oh, I see now! Well this is weird,
and certainly won't be fun.

I don't really know what's happening.
This all must be some mistake!
Why are they all floating over here,
while offering us some CAKE!?

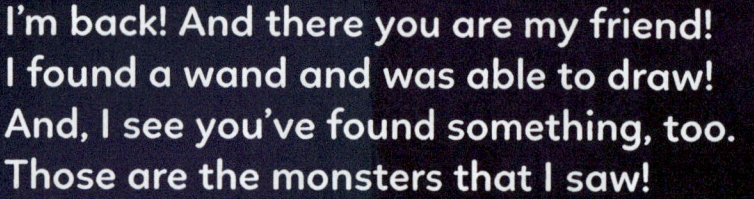

Whoa! They're not really monsters at all!
They're just ghosts in disguise!
That explains the creepy costume
and all those spooky eyes.

But why would you all hide like that
and cause me so much fear?
Oh my! It's all coming back now.
Suddenly everything is clear!

I was here with all of them,
when I first found that magic book.
I really shouldn't have touched it,
but I just had to take a look.

A spell was cast, my memory lost,
and I was cursed to roam.
They're not just ghosts, they're family,
and this was once my home!

They say they used costumes to fit in,
just hoping I might appear.
Because that's how little humans
often dress this time of year!

They never gave up searching!
Each year, they'd try, just in case.
On the chance that they might find me,
and bring me home to this very place!

I'm so happy to see everyone.
I want you to meet my special friend.
We've been on quite an adventure,
which I fear is coming to an end.

I'm very sad. I'm going to miss you!
You've helped to set me free!
Wait! What's that you say?
You'd like to
Draw Something Just For Me?

Draw Something For The Ghost!

I'll cherish your gift forever,
and I'll never forget this night!
I started out so uncertain,
and you helped to ease my fright.

I knew that we would get along,
and you could also tell.
Finding a friend you really like
is the most magical kind of spell.

So, I guess we've solved this mystery
and must surely say goodbye.
I'm feeling rather emotional now,
but I won't start to cry.

I've learned that I have powers too,
with all the help you gave.
Even though I might be small,
I found I could be brave!

And you've inspired me to use that real magic I have inside! Making things appear from scratch, fills me with such pride!

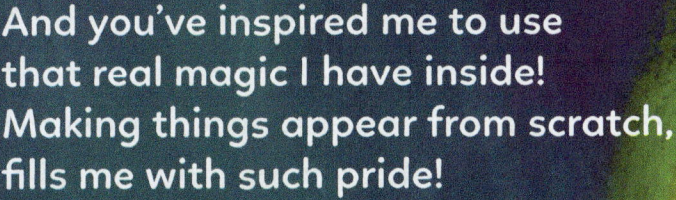

DRAW WHAT THE GHOST IMAGINED!

I'm not sure that I'll ever be able to draw the things you drew. But if I keep right on drawing, I'll be an **ARTIST** just like you!

About The Author

Charlie O'Shields is the creator of Doodlewash®, host of the Sketching Stuff podcast, and a big kid at heart. For 2,000 consecutive days he created a little watercolor illustration in his sketchbook and shared a rambling story about whatever came to mind that day. A selection of those stories and illustrations were published in his book: "Sketching Stuff: Stories Sketched From Life".

In 2016, he founded World Watercolor Month in July, an annual charitable event supporting arts education, featuring the 31 watercolors in 31 days challenge, which welcomes people from all over the globe at any skill level, using any method or style of watercolor painting or coloring they love most!

His true passion is inspiring as many people as possible to draw and color and help artists of all ages reconnect with their inner child, natural creativity, and just have tons of fun!

Love To Draw And Color?

Visit me at SketchingStuff.com to learn more!

Printed in the USA
CPSIA information can be obtained
at www.ICGtesting.com
LVHW050727221023
761786LV00006B/55